J

White-Collar Crime

CRIME, JUSTICE, AND PUNISHMENT

White-Collar Crime

Gina De Angelis

Austin Sarat, GENERAL EDITOR

CHELSEA HOUSE PUBLISHERS
Philadelphia

Frontis: *The future of white-collar crime lies inside the technology of tomorrow.*

Chelsea House Publishers
Editor in Chief Stephen Reginald
Managing Editor James D. Gallagher
Production Manager Pamela Loos
Art Director Sara Davis
Director of Photography Judy L. Hasday
Senior Production Editor LeeAnne Gelletly

Staff for WHITE-COLLAR CRIME
Associate Art Director Takeshi Takahashi
Cover Illustrator Sara Davis

First Printing

1 3 5 7 9 8 6 4 2

The Chelsea House World Wide Web site address is
http://www.chelseahouse.com

Library of Congress Cataloging-in-Publication Data

De Angelis, Gina
White-collar crime / Gina De Angelis.
    p. cm. — (Crime, justice, and punishment)
Includes bibliographical references and index.
Summary: Discusses such white-collar crimes as fraud, computer crimes, and insider stock trading and how these crimes should be deterred and punished.

ISBN 0-7910-4279-0 (hc)

1. White-collar crimes—Juvenile literature. 2. Commercial crimes—Juvenile literature. 3. Computer crimes—Juvenile literature. 4. Fraud—Juvenile literature. 5. Criminal justice, Administration of—Juvenile literature.
[1. White-collar crime.] I. Title. II. Series.
HV6768.D42   1999
364.16'8—dc21   99-26299
                                            CIP

Contents

CRIME, JUSTICE, AND PUNISHMENT

Fears and Fascinations:

An Introduction to
Crime, Justice, and Punishment

By Austin Sarat

We live with crime and images of crime all around us. Crime evokes in most of us a deep aversion, a feeling of profound vulnerability, but it also evokes an equally deep fascination. Today, in major American cities the fear of crime is a major fact of life, some would say a disproportionate response to the realities of crime. Yet the fear of crime is real, palpable in the quickened steps and furtive glances of people walking down darkened streets. At the same time, we eagerly follow crime stories on television and in movies. We watch with a "who done it" curiosity, eager to see the illicit deed done, the investigation undertaken, the miscreant brought to justice and given his just deserts. On the streets the presence of crime is a reminder of our own vulnerability and the precariousness of our taken-for-granted rights and freedoms. On television and in the movies the crime story gives us a chance to probe our own darker motives, to ask "Is there a criminal within?" as well as to feel the collective satisfaction of seeing justice done.

Fear and fascination, these two poles of our engagement with crime, are, of course, only part of the story. Crime is, after all, a major social and legal problem, not just an issue of our individual psychology. Politicians today use our fear of, and fascination with, crime for political advantage. How we respond to crime, as well as to the political uses of the crime issue, tells us a lot about who we are as a people as well as what we value and what we tolerate. Is our response compassionate or severe? Do we seek to understand or to punish, to enact an angry vengeance or to rehabilitate and welcome the criminal back into our midst? The CRIME, JUSTICE, AND PUNISHMENT series is designed to explore these themes, to ask why we are fearful and fascinated, to probe the meanings and motivations of crimes and criminals and of our responses to them, and, finally, to ask what we can learn about ourselves and the society in which we live by examining our responses to crime.

Crime is always a challenge to the prevailing normative order and a test of the values and commitments of law-abiding people. It is sometimes a Raskolnikov-like act of defiance, an assertion of the unwillingness of some to live according to the rules of conduct laid out by organized society. In this sense, crime marks the limits of the law and reminds us of law's all-too-regular failures. Yet sometimes there is more desperation than defiance in criminal acts; sometimes they signal a deep pathology or need in the criminal. To confront crime is thus also to come face-to-face with the reality of social difference, of class privilege and extreme deprivation, of race and racism, of children neglected, abandoned, or abused whose response is to enact on others what they have experienced themselves. And occasionally crime, or what is labeled a criminal act, represents a call for justice, an appeal to a higher moral order against the inadequacies of existing law.

Figuring out the meaning of crime and the motivations of criminals and whether crime arises from defiance, desperation, or the appeal for justice is never an easy task. The motivations and meanings of crime are as varied as are the persons who engage in criminal conduct. They are as mysterious as any of the mysteries of the human soul. Yet the desire to know the secrets of crime and the criminal is a strong one, for in that knowledge may lie one step on the road to protection, if not an assurance of one's own personal safety. Nonetheless, as strong as that desire may be, there is no available technology that can allow us to know the whys of crime with much confidence, let alone a scientific certainty. We can, however, capture something about crime by studying the defiance, desperation, and quest for justice that may be associated with it. Books in the Crime, Justice, and Punishment series will take up that challenge. They tell stories of crime and criminals, some famous, most not, some glamorous and exciting, most mundane and commonplace.

This series will, in addition, take a sober look at American criminal justice, at the procedures through which we investigate crimes and identify criminals, at the institutions in which innocence or guilt is determined. In these procedures and institutions we confront the thrill of the chase as well as the challenge of protecting the rights of those who defy our laws. It is through the efficiency and dedication of law enforcement that we might capture the criminal; it is in the rare instances of their corruption or brutality that we feel perhaps our deepest betrayal. Police, prosecutors, defense lawyers, judges, and jurors administer criminal justice and in their daily actions give substance to the guarantees of the Bill of Rights. What is an adversarial system of justice? How does it work? Why do we have it? Books in the Crime, Justice, and Punishment series will examine the thrill of the chase as we seek to capture the criminal. They will also reveal the drama and majesty of the criminal trial as well as the day-to-day reality of a criminal justice system in which trials are the exception and negotiated pleas of guilty are the rule.

When the trial is over or the plea has been entered, when we have separated the innocent from the guilty, the moment of punishment has arrived. The injunction to punish the guilty, to respond to pain inflicted by inflicting pain, is as old as civilization itself. "An eye for an eye and a tooth for a tooth" is a biblical reminder that punishment must measure pain for pain. But our response to the criminal must be better than and different from the crime itself. The biblical admonition, along with the constitutional prohibition of "cruel and unusual punishment," signals that we seek to punish justly and to be just not only in the determination of who can and should be punished, but in how we punish as well. But neither reminder tells us what to do with the wrongdoer. Do we rape the rapist, or burn the home of the arsonist? Surely justice and decency say no. But, if not, then how can and should we punish? In a world in which punishment is neither identical to the crime nor an automatic response to it, choices must be made and we must make them. Books in the CRIME, JUSTICE, AND PUNISHMENT series will examine those choices and the practices, and politics, of punishment. How do we punish and why do we punish as we do? What can we learn about the rationality and appropriateness of today's responses to crime by examining our past and its responses? What works? Is there, and can there be, a just measure of pain?

CRIME, JUSTICE, AND PUNISHMENT brings together books on some of the great themes of human social life. The books in this series capture our fear and fascination with crime and examine our responses to it. They remind us of the deadly seriousness of these subjects. They bring together themes in law, literature, and popular culture to challenge us to think again, to think anew, about subjects that go to the heart of who we are and how we can and will live together.

*   *   *   *   *

Far from the ordinary image of the predatory criminal who uses violence or the threat of violence to violate the law, white-collar crime is always nonviolent. For the white-collar criminal, fraud, misrepresentation, duplicity, and manipulation are the crucial tools of the trade. White-collar crime, in fact, may be defined by either the means used in the perpetration of the offense or by the status of the offender, and most commonly it involves both: a relatively high status offender using nonviolent means to commit some kind of theft. Thus white-collar crime challenges traditional understandings of crime as arising from the desperate circumstances of society's most disadvantaged members. And, in the face of white-collar crime, one may be tempted to ask why relatively well-off people would resort to criminality. The answer, of course, is sometimes need, sometimes relative deprivation, and sometimes pure greed.

White-Collar Crime provides a comprehensive overview of both traditional kinds of white-collar offenses and innovative kinds of criminality made available by new technologies. Through a careful marshaling of historical evidence and individual case studies, this book shows what motivates white-collar criminals as well as how they operate. It documents the massive damage that is done by white-collar crime—from large-scale swindles to political corruption. It also describes the way that white-collar criminals have been punished, and it reminds us of the disparities between the way we deal with street criminals and their higher-status counterparts. This book demonstrates the challenges that white-collar crime poses for law enforcement and for a criminal justice system dedicated to equal justice. It is the kind of book that will leave its readers better informed and better able to think about ways of responding to those challenges.

CRIMINALS WITH CLEAN FINGERNAILS

When you hear the word *criminal* or *convict*, what kind of person do you think of? Do you think of a man in a three-piece business suit who works in a skyscraper on Wall Street and who keeps pictures of his wife and children in his office? Do you think of the teller at your bank, or an accountant? Do you think of a teenager whose hobby is computers, or the housewife next door, or your state representative, or your family doctor? Probably not. Yet, these people can be capable of committing crimes that cost others millions of dollars.

Edwin Sutherland, a criminologist, coined the term *white-collar criminal* in an attempt to describe criminals from higher socioeconomic levels. He thought that certain crimes were being committed by persons whom no one would suspect of criminal behavior—professionals called "white-collar" workers, such as bankers, lawyers, or public officials (people who would wear a white collar to work, as opposed to the blue shirt and overalls of

This will probably be the preferred modus operandi of white-collar criminals in the 21st century.

13

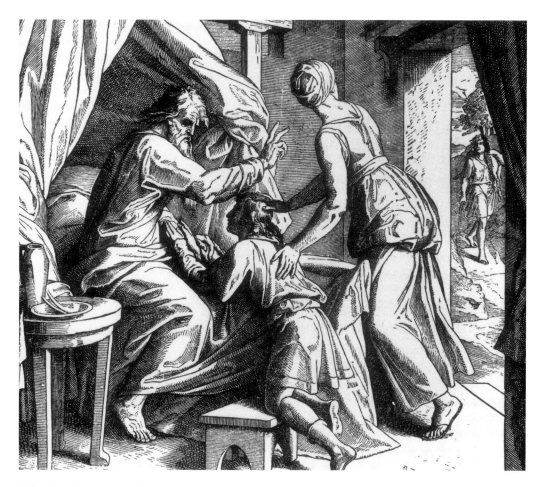

When Jacob impersonated Esau to gain his first-born inheritance, was it a case of ancient "white-collar" crime?

the "blue-collar" worker). Sutherland wanted a phrase to point out that not all criminals fit the stereotypical picture that most people have in their minds. White-collar crimes are committed by professional workers from the worlds of banking and finance, stocks and bonds, politics and government, and even science and art. They are "criminals with clean fiingernails," who have the ability and the access to commit crimes through cheating, dishonesty, or corruption. White-collar crimes of forgery, fraud, tax evasion, blackmail, and bribery have existed for as long as people have owned property or objects, and as long as other people have not owned but wanted property or objects. In other words, crimes that we now call white collar have always existed.

In the Bible, in Genesis, chapter 27, Jacob impersonates his elder brother, Esau, to trick his blind father into giving Jacob the inheritance that is Esau's birthright. Today, what Jacob did could be called a form of white-collar crime. His deception did not involve physical injury or the threat of it, but it did result in injury to both his brother and his father. So also could other crimes mentioned in the Bible's New Testament, where examples abound of tax collectors who were cheats. There are also numerous references throughout history and literature to "quacks" and "charlatans"— people who claimed to be something they were not— and under today's definition they would also be white-collar criminals.

Today the term *white-collar crime* has lost much of its original meaning. It no longer refers exclusively to crimes committed by high-status offenders but tends to mean any nonviolent crime, sometimes also called "victimless" or "economic" crime.

To a large extent computers have leveled the criminal playing field. Their wide availability has given criminals of all socioeconomic groups a powerful tool for committing white-collar crimes. Most computer crimes do not involve violence. They play on greed, pride, or some unique characteristic of the victim. These crimes are based on dishonesty, not force. One police officer who specializes in computer crime remarked that "the average guy we arrest has got a college degree. They plot and plan. That takes a lot more skill" than, for example, armed robbery. As millions of people all over the world gain access to high technology, white-collar crimes can be committed by almost anyone with the will to break the law. Nearly all white-collar crimes involve the use of computers or telecommunications, according to Vic Sussman of *U.S. News and World Report.*

Phreakers can use phone lines to disrupt communications and steal phone time—a crime that usually goes undetected until the bill arrives.

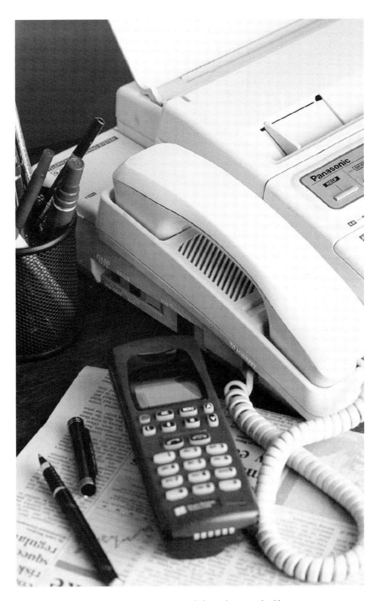

the hard way when its monthly phone bill, a staggering $200,000, arrived in a box instead of an envelope."

A similar form of computer crime is perpetrated by phone "phreakers," or hackers. Instead of accessing computer systems, phreakers break into voice-mail systems. One incident involved the New York City Police Department. Phreakers broke into the NYPD's voice-mail system and changed the message that greeted callers. The new recording said that officers were too busy eating doughnuts and drinking coffee to answer the phones and directed callers to dial 119 in an emergency.

Often voice-mail break-ins involve more than pranks and can cost companies a great deal of money. For example, sometimes hackers break into the voice-mail systems of companies that have established toll-free numbers for their customers. These hackers then set up their own voice mailboxes. This gives them free voice mail and long-distance phone calls, all at the company's expense. In some cases hackers even broadcast the information over the Internet. Walt Manning, a former police officer who now works as a security consultant in Texas, said he had a client who lost $4.5 million over a three-day period from this kind of computer break-in.

In 1993, three men in California reprogrammed the telephone lines of three different radio stations to prevent any calls but their own from reaching the stations during a contest. At their trial, the men pleaded guilty to charges of computer fraud. They had received over $20,000 cash, two Porsches, and two vacations in Hawaii by being the "right" callers to the stations.

Not all hackers violate computer security for their own profit. Robert Morris was convicted in 1990 of disrupting the Internet. But Morris, a young graduate student in computer science, was running an experiment. He had written a network computer program designed to enter the network to see how many computers it could reach. No data was destroyed, and Morris did not access any classified information. Author Katie Hafner believes that Morris was a high-profile scapegoat, convicted of a crime to set an example. "The Morris case captured the most publicity of all computer crime cases and brought out the nation's collective anxiety about computer hackers," Hafner declared.

Robert Morris's experiment at breaking into computers as a graduate student landed him in prison.

As more computers become connected to each other and as all of us operate in an increasingly "cashless" society, computer crimes will increase. Law enforcement organizations will struggle to keep ahead of "cyber criminals" by creating and enforcing computer security.

Law enforcement is already catching up to hackers in computer literacy. In 1996, the FBI caught Leslie Rogge, one of its Ten Most Wanted Fugitives. Rogge was caught when an Internet user in Guatemala recognized Rogge as a man he had seen in a photo posted on the FBI's World Wide Web site. In 1997, when a teenager in Illinois was kidnapped and there were no leads, the suspect was captured because a computer-savvy police officer searched the boy's computer files. The officer discovered electronic mail correspondence with Richard Romero, a man from Florida. Romero and the boy were later found in Kentucky, and Romero was arrested and charged.

Sometimes even amateur computer users have tracked hackers. In March 1997, two college students were able to trace a hacker and notify authorities within three hours of the crime. In this case, the hacker had vandalized the website of the National Collegiate Athletic Association (NCAA). The two students, Jay Kamm, at Duke University in North Carolina, and Benjamin DeLong, at the University of Massachusetts, did not know each other, but worked together via electronic mail to track the hacker through clues in his "cybergraffiti." The clues led to the address of a particular computer. DeLong and Kamm wrote a four-page report of their findings, which they gave to the NCAA the next morning.

Laws have been vague about computer crimes. How can computer criminals be charged with a crime when there are few laws stating what the crime is? Rich Bernes, an FBI agent in California, asks, "Suppose someone accesses your computer and downloads files. What should she be charged with? Burglary or trespassing? Wire fraud or copyright violation?" Who handles the prosecution of these criminals? Should law enforcement agencies have the right to break into people's files while investigating cases of cyber crime? If not, how can they build a case?

Many local police departments do not have the funds or personnel to run a special force devoted to investigating cyber crimes, but the number of police officers and detectives familiar with computers and the tracking of these criminals increases daily.

At the national level, specific agencies monitor

One of the FBI's Ten Most Wanted Fugitives in 1996, Leslie Rogge was finally caught with the help of the Internet.

businesses vulnerable to white-collar crimes or the crimes themselves. The Secret Service covers the credit industry, telephone services, and the federal Treasury Department. The FBI investigates industrial espionage, bank fraud, organized crime, and terrorism. The FBI also has the National Computer Crime Squad (NCCS), which is responsible for investigating violations of the Federal Computer Fraud and Abuse Act of 1986. This act covers computer break-ins that cross state or international borders, that involve intruding into federal or state computers, or that involve accessing financial or medical records. The NCCS also investigates any break-ins of telephone companies or other major computer networks, industrial espionage, and computer software piracy. Pirated software and stolen computer components are estimated to cause annual losses of over $24 billion worldwide.

As with other crimes, the best way to prevent white-collar crime is to make others aware of the methods and abilities of the criminals. Computer security firms are springing up around the world to aid businesses and individuals trying to "lock the doors" of their computer systems.

Computer crimes, because they are high-tech, are news-grabbing stories. But not all white-collar crimes are committed by computer, and white-collar crime was around long before the computer was invented. There have always been those who were willing to use any kind of trickery to cheat others—the computer has just given them a new high-tech weapon. Although the term *white-collar crime* was coined to emphasize the upper- or middle-class origins of certain criminals, the use of cunning and intelligence instead of force is what distinguishes the white-collar criminal of today.

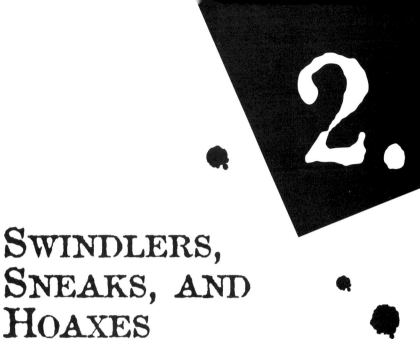

SWINDLERS, SNEAKS, AND HOAXES

From the beginning of the banking and finance industry, which was established in Italy in the 14th century, economic systems have become more and more complex. Economic crimes have also become very complicated.

An example of how one man swindled thousands out of their money occurred in 18th-century France. In this case, financial speculation ruined many people who invested in a financial "bubble." The government of France was heavily indebted in 1717 when a Scottish gambler named John Law was permitted to take over the government's debt. The people and companies holding IOUs from the government gave them to Law, and they received stock in Law's Mississippi Company in return. The company had a monopoly, or exclusive

The floor of the New York Stock Exchange, where the desire to make large amounts of money quickly can lead to corruption.

rights, of trade to France's colonies in the lower valley of the Mississippi. Law promised to pay dividends on the stock from his company's profits from this trade. As more people bought stock in Law's company, the price for each share rose. Soon stock speculation took over. More people would buy stocks in the hope that the value would continue to go up. The price per share became so high that the stockholders began to fear that they would never earn enough in stock dividends to recover their costs for the shares. So they began to sell. Suddenly, everyone wanted to sell and the price for each share plummeted. Those who had gone into debt to buy shares soon found that they had worthless stock on their hands in addition to their debts.

In England, a similar situation of stock speculation occurred when the government of Britain allowed the South Sea Company to assume its debt. The company had a trading monopoly in South America and the Pacific islands. But like the "Mississippi Bubble," the "South Sea Bubble" burst in 1720. Both events prompted government regulation of stock trading.

Many social changes took place during the Industrial Revolution of the 19th century. Large factories replaced many small shops. The factories could produce consumer goods faster and cheaper than could artisans and crafts-men. People began to leave farms and small towns to go to cities where factory jobs could be found. Travel and mobility became a feature of industrialized societies. With mobility came more chances for "imposture"—pretend-ing to be someone else for unlawful purposes.

One famous example of imposture and fraud came to light in 1873. Four Americans managed to bilk the Bank of England out of the modern equivalent of about $4 million. The men were Austin Bidwell, his brother George, Austin's friend and forger George Macdonnell, and, later, another friend named Edwin Noyes. They concocted an elaborate plan involving careful impos-ture, excellent forgery, extensive "casing" or spying,

John Law swindled numerous people in a "bubble" scheme, while supposedly helping the French government with its heavy debt.

and money laundering. Over the course of two years, they successfully carried out their scheme.

The Americans began by presenting themselves as well-to-do businessmen. Austin Bidwell was tall, handsome, well dressed, and charming. He could easily make himself look the part of an important and wealthy businessman. But Bidwell did not have a permanent address. He would have to charm someone into vouching for his character and background. The men also had enough money to play their roles. They needed large amounts of money to dress well, to win the trust of bank officials, accountants, and men who served as references. Money was also needed to purchase the proper materials for forgery and to pay for travel to and from England, Europe, South America, and the United States.

Austin called himself Frederick Albert Warren and Charles Johnson Horton, among other aliases. George Bidwell posed as Captain Bradshaw. And George Macdonnell became Mr. Mapleson. The fourth thief, Edwin Noyes, would join them later.

The first part of the plan was based on obtaining bank letters of credit, which were like modern blank checks. George Bidwell and George Macdonnell would buy legitimate letters of credit from banks in England, Europe, or even South America. Brazil was ideal because of the great distance between it and Europe. They would have a longer time before frauds on Brazilian banks would be discovered.

MacDonnell would make excellently forged copies of letters of credit in the names of the fake identities. The men would then take the letters to other banks and in a series of small transactions withdraw money. The bank officials accepted the forgeries as authentic and expected to receive the amount disbursed from the original, issuing bank. Before the bankers found out this would not happen, the men would have moved on to another city, using new aliases. Austin would deposit the stolen money in his (Mr. Warren's) account at the Bank of England.

Meanwhile the forgers looked for another loophole in European business procedures. Banks in England also used letters of exchange. A letter of exchange is also like a modern bank check, but with the amount of money filled in. The letter of exchange would order a bank to release money to the person identified on the document. This order is the "Pay to the order of" part

25

HORACE HOVAN,
ALIAS LITTLE HORACE,
BANK SNEAK.

26

AUGUSTUS RAYMOND,
ALIAS GUS RAYMOND.
SNEAK AND FORGER.

27

FRANK BUCK,
ALIAS BUCKY TAYLOR.
BANK SNEAK.

28

JOHN TRACY,
ALIAS BIG TRACY, ALIAS REILLY.
PICKPOCKET,
BURGLAR & SECOND STORY MAN.

29

CHARLES WILSON,
ALIAS LITTLE PAUL.
SNEAK AND SHOP LIFTER.

30

DAVID GOLDSTEIN,
ALIAS SHEENY DAVE,
SNEAK AND SHOP LIFTER

A poster of some of 1890's most-wanted white-collar criminals.

of a modern check. In England in the 1870s, letters of exchange were honored by banks before the bank confirmed that the letter of exchange was real because verifying the letter of exchange took up to three months. The impostors could present forged bills of exchange to the Bank of England, make withdrawals on them, and not be discovered for three months.

In December 1872, George Bidwell cabled his friend Edwin Noyes in New York. Noyes came to London and agreed to help for 5 percent of the take. The men carefully staged "Mr. Horton" (Austin) hiring Mr. Noyes as his confidential clerk. They put an ad in the paper, interviewed in front of hotel staff, and had a legal contract drawn up. Noyes could claim that he was hired by a Mr. Horton and had no connection to the others. Noyes was to act as Mr. Horton's deputy at London's Continental Bank. He would be able to withdraw Mr. Horton's money—which was, of course, in the form of checks drawn on the phony Mr. F. A. Warren's account at the Bank of England.

Around January 1, 1873, Mr. Warren explained that he would be out of town on an extended business trip and would conduct his bank deposits and withdrawals by registered mail. Throughout all this time, the impostors cycled the same fake letters of exchange and letters of credit through Banks in England, France, Germany, and Holland.

Whenever the men used genuine bills of exchange or checks, Macdonnell would forge perfect copies and leave the amounts and dates blank. After they were filled in, George Bidwell—purporting to be F. A. Warren on business in Birmingham—sent the forgeries, for varying amounts, to the Bank of England by mail. Meanwhile, Mr. Horton's "confidential clerk," Edwin Noyes, in London had blank checks in the name of F. A. Warren. Noyes used them to transfer money to Mr. Horton's account at Continental Bank, from which Noyes, as Mr. Horton's assistant, could withdraw the funds. To cover the tracks of the enormous transactions, Noyes then converted the money into gold, various foreign currencies, or U.S. bonds. After a few weeks of this business, George Bidwell planned for them all to be out of the country, well before the three-month window closed and the first forged bills were discovered.

At the end of February 1873, the con men had made nearly £80,000. With the fruits of their near-perfect crime in their pockets, greed undid the American swindlers. As the con men prepared to leave England, Macdonnell could not bear to throw away the rest of his elegant forgeries of bank notes and letters of exchange. So he chose two dozen of the remaining notes and presented them to the Bank of England. Were these final notes honored, the Americans would have added another £26,265 to their haul. But in his haste, Macdonnell failed to put dates on two of his fake notes. When bank officials in London investigated the incomplete documents, they realized that the bank had no record of these notes. When the bankers smelled fraud, the perfect crime was discovered.

Noyes was caught when he went to withdraw from Mr. Horton's account at the Bank of England. Macdonnell was caught before disembarking in New York from a ship he had hopped in Le Havre, France, in early March 1873. Austin Bidwell was arrested in Havana, Cuba, within three weeks. George Bidwell was finally caught in April. All four were found guilty and sentenced to life in prison.

The men very nearly pulled off their plan without a hitch. The case illustrates the ease with which enormous frauds can be committed against too-gullible people, with a lot of planning on the part of intelligent white-collar perpetrators.

During the Industrial Revolution, goods became cheaper and more plentiful. Factories produced con-

Industrialist Henry Ford was taken in by a con man claiming to have made fuel from water in 1916.

sumer goods almost too fast, producing more goods than people could buy. So to keep selling, businessmen had to think of ways to make people replace perfectly good items that they had bought only recently.

As a result, advertising became more sneaky. It was designed to appeal to thousands of people, selling them items they probably did not need. Advertisers often told outright lies to sell their products, or took money for goods that had never existed and then skipped town before the victims could find out.

There were many traveling peddlers who were not always the poor, hardworking souls they pretended to be. One large clan of traveling swindlers in the United States was known as the Williamsons. The first Williamson arrived in New York from Scotland in the 1890s. He and his large family made a living by traveling throughout the country selling shoddy goods with fake brand names.

The Williamsons also perpetrated scams such as installing fake lightning rods on houses, or offering to paint houses and barns for a cut rate and then using watered-down paint. Scams like these are among the oldest of what we now call white-collar crime, and they still manage to find victims.

Faced with a world of consumer items such as had never been seen before, and with advertising creating the desire to own more and more goods, many previously honest people were lured into criminal behavior.

During the Victorian era such behavior was often excused because of the widespread belief in a mental illness called kleptomania. However when poor people committed crimes, there was an easy answer—they were not well-off or were ill-bred. Kleptomania was an illness that supposedly explained why well-off people—particularly women—would commit theft or fraud.

Four middle-class, respectable women of Lynn, Massachusetts, "amassed 'Trunkfuls of Booty' before they were caught in 1897," says Elaine Abelson, author of *When Ladies Go A-Thieving*. Newspapers, doctors, and society in general often concluded that women, because of their weak natures, were unable to resist temptations posed by department store displays and advertising. But Abelson notes that these four women simply wanted a lot of things they could not afford. The fact that they "amassed Trunkfuls of Booty" suggests that their crimes involved careful planning.

A caricature of millionaire J. P. Morgan in Life *magazine, 1902.*

Great advances in the sciences also took place during the 1800s. Charles Darwin's theory of evolution was published in 1859. The first dinosaur fossils were discovered. Thomas Edison, Alexander Graham Bell, and Guglielmo Marconi produced the electric light, the telephone, and early radio in the latter half of that century. At the same time, Pierre and Marie Curie were discovering radioactivity. Karl Marx and Friedrich Engels were composing their great social and economic theories, and Sigmund Freud was laying the foundations of modern psychiatry. The world was changing rapidly, and knowledge was becoming more specialized. The rapidly expanding boundaries of human knowledge enabled some dishonest people to perpetrate elaborate scientific and scholarly hoaxes.

In the fall of 1869, it was reported that the petrified remains of a human giant had been found on a farm in New York State. Hundreds of people came and paid to see the fossilized "Cardiff Giant," as it came to be called. The receipts for admission were so huge that it was decided to take the sculpture on tour. Several well-respected professors were taken in by the realistically old appearance of the limestone giant. It was marked with channels and pocks, which would have taken centuries of running water to have carved in the extremely hard limestone of the area. No one was allowed to touch the giant though. When a competent expert finally did manage to get a piece of the statue, he realized why the Cardiff Giant appeared to be so old. The hard "limestone" was actually gypsum, a very soft material, that had been shipped in from Iowa. The giant was a fake.

In 1916 another scientific hoax reportedly fooled the American automobile manufacturer Henry Ford. A 70-year-old man named Louis Enricht claimed to have created from water a fuel similar to gasoline. Enricht refused to divulge the secret of his magic green liquid, until he had managed to receive competing offers from several large companies with a huge interest in buying the formula. He was visited at his home by Henry Ford, who gave Enricht an automobile and offered him $1,000 cash and a contract. The formula proved to be a hoax. Enricht was finally sentenced to prison after attempting to cash in with a few similar hoaxes. He was paroled in 1924 and died penniless shortly thereafter.

The late 19th century was the era of the great "robber barons" like millionaires Andrew Carnegie, John D. Rockefeller, and J. P. Morgan. There were no laws against monopolizing entire industries and destroying all competition. There were no safe food laws and no government regulations restricting businessmen to fair business practices. The Carnegies, Rockefellers, and Morgans of the world had the money and the power to control government. This was the time of white-collar crime by multimillionaires. Many similar titans were able to achieve wealth and power by cheating or buying out competitors, by bribing or blackmailing public officials, or by committing what would become violations of government antitrust regulations. Mark Twain referred to this period between 1880 and 1910 as the Gilded Age.

The administration of President Ulysses S. Grant is particularly well-known for corruption, mostly because he appointed dishonest people who accepted bribes and

Five of the witnesses in the "Teapot Dome" scandal that rocked the U.S. government in 1924. From left to right: Rear Admiral Gregory, Admiral J. T. Latimer, Representative William B. Oliver, Representative Fred Butler, and Admiral J. K. Robinson.

Charles Ponzi being released from prison after serving seven years for defrauding thousands of investors.

defrauded the treasury of tax moneys. But Grant's administration was not the only one affected by white-collar crime. The federal government in the later decades of the 19th century and the first few decades of the 20th took steps to pass legislation that controlled widespread corruption in business and politics. Crime continued, however, at the highest levels.

During Warren Harding's administration in the 1920s, the federal government was rocked by the "Teapot Dome" oil scandals. Teapot Dome was the name of government-owned oil fields near Casper, Wyoming, that had been illegally leased to private developers. Several highly placed government officials were implicated, and the trials took several years. The Secretary of the Navy was eventually forced to resign in 1924 and the Secretary of the Interior, Albert B. Fall, was convicted of accepting huge bribes.

Also in the 1920s, an Italian-American named Charles Ponzi took advantage of the raucous business world. He began selling shares in a company that he said was investing in Spanish mail coupons. He promised his investors an outrageously high return on their investment in a very short period of time. As word spread, people wanted to invest their money with Ponzi. The second wave of investors gave Ponzi the funds to pay off the first wave, and so on. Ponzi was a millionaire—for a while. Most of his investors were other Italian-American immigrants and working-class people. They were proud of Ponzi's ability to make it in the business world. They saw him as a living example of America as the land of opportunity.

But reporters and accountants soon became interested in Ponzi and in how he was able to achieve such wealth so quickly. A little investigation revealed that Ponzi was not the business-savvy financier that he appeared to be. But people kept investing. Finally his account books were examined and the lie was exposed. Ponzi caused such an uproar that his name has been attached to the style of con he perpetrated—the "Ponzi scheme." Charles Ponzi's scheme was a fine example of a white-collar investment scam.

Recently, a *New York Times* article stated that there has been a new twist on old investment scams—an "affinity scheme." In these kinds of schemes, the "con artists and their victims are linked by religion or ethnic background." Like the investors who bought into Ponzi's scheme, the victims believe their money is safe with that person or company, because their own countryman, or fellow believer, wouldn't defraud them. "In the last five years," the article states, "the SEC has investigated affinity fraud schemes in which Indian, Polish, Salvadoran, Chinese, and Vietnamese immigrants have been defrauded of millions by fellow immigrants."

And so the styles of crime that we call white collar continue to be perpetrated. In the words of George Young of the Cincinnati Better Business Bureau, "As long as people delude themselves that goods or services can be bought at less than a fair price," or that it is possible to get rich quickly without working, crimes that play off greed will succeed.

3.

CORPORATE, GOVERNMENT, AND ORGANIZED GREED

Corporate and government crimes are a worldwide problem involving large sums of money, political bribery, industrial espionage, and widespread corruption at top levels. The infiltration of organized crime into some local governments and businesses increases the extent and seriousness of many of these white-collar crimes.

One man who combined corporate and government corruption was the "Swedish Match King," Ivar Kreuger. The founder of a match company in Sweden in 1913, Kreuger would eventually take part in many crimes that enabled him to steal millions of dollars. He forged bonds and certificates and he falsified account books. He used these counterfeits to gain huge amounts of credit and loans from governments and banks. He built monopolies in several countries (which is not always illegal, although it is in the United States). He created companies that did not exist.

Kreuger would use a dummy phone that he could

Ivar Kreuger conned thousands of government officials and investors out of what added up to over $1 billion.

make ring with a foot pedal, to get out of answering difficult questions or to impress visitors. His wealth and manner made him very attractive to women, whom he bribed to keep quiet about his many affairs. Although he owned several legitimate match factories, Kreuger's enormous financial empire was built on credit with real assets of a much lower value.

The stock market crash on October 29, 1929, was the beginning of Kreuger's end. The Great Depression dried up credit, and Kreuger's business scams had lived on easy credit. Still, he managed to keep up the facade of success until 1932, when his account books were finally examined by outsiders. Kreuger then shot himself.

Ivar Kreuger's bankruptcy resulted in debts of over $1 billion. Among his creditors were many American investors, who lost an estimated $98 million. Banks and many governments also lost millions.

Government and corporate greed can cause more than just economic loss. On January 28, 1986, as millions watched on television, the space shuttle *Challenger* lifted off to suddenly explode into a fireball in the sky. Later investigation would show that a government agency and a private corporation had been aware of a dangerous flaw in the space shuttle but had not reported it. The President's Commission in 1986 concluded that the fault lay with both NASA and Morton-Thiokol, Inc., the company that built the flawed solid-rocket boosters.

In the months before the fateful launch, Morton-Thiokol was trying to have its contract with NASA renewed. Officials may have felt that admitting a mistake would jeopardize the renewal of the Morton-Thiokol contract. The misconduct that resulted in the explosion of the *Challenger*, says author Ronald Kramer, "can be viewed as an instance of state-corporate crime."

Because the two organizations worked together to design and build the *Challenger*, and because both organizations should have caught the mistake before it became a catastrophe, both were found negligent.

Not all white-collar, corporate greed ends with spectacular fireballs like the space shuttle *Challenger*. But winning contracts for goods or services from the United States government—the largest business on earth—is fertile ground for corporate scams and for

The explosion of the Challenger shook the world as well as the company that made the defective equipment.

unlawfully rigging the game against honest businesses.

To obtain a government contract, companies are required to bid in secret—to submit their proposed plan for the project, including an estimated cost. Some companies participate in the illegal practice of "collusion in bidding" or "bid-fixing," which is an agreement by bidders not to go lower or higher than a certain price.

The Small Business Administration (SBA) was established in 1953 to help support small companies. It also helps ensure that a fair proportion of United States government contracts go to small businesses. According to author August Bequai, though, the SBA is "riddled with fraud." "Shell" companies are created by other, large businesses, which hire a "front man" to pose as the chief executive officer (CEO). In this way the "shell" company can receive a government contract that is intended for a small business but that is really filled by the larger business, which also gets the money.

Other examples of illegal corporate actions that cheat the government and all taxpayers include padding costs, delivering shoddy work, and filing false claims for nonexistent expenses. For example, one doctor billed Medicaid for 43 comprehensive examinations involving only one patient, and a dentist filed a claim with Medicaid for performing a prostate procedure.

Unfortunately, social welfare programs, established to help people get the food, health care, and money they need to survive, are full of fraudulent claims. People sell or counterfeit food stamps, or use "ghost payrolls" to get federal money for nonexistent employees. Abuse of social welfare programs has cost the government billions of dollars.

Widespread corruption of politicians and public officials show up in the form of bribes, kickbacks, and political fraud. Bribes can involve domestic or foreign elements, public officials or private individuals, and small or large amounts of money. Political bribes are "gifts" offered to government employees or elected offi-

The mayor of Lawrence, Massachusetts, demonstrates the electronic facial and imaging card designed to combat welfare fraud.

cials in return for administrative or political favors. Political bribery is not limited to public figures in this country. Foreign elements often bribe U.S. officials or businessmen, and vice versa.

A kickback occurs when a politician agrees to help grant a government contract to a certain company. He or she knows that the company will overcharge the government for its services and "kick back" a percentage of the profit to the politician. In some large cities, businesses cannot obtain city or state government contracts without "kicking back." Often organized crime is involved, making the whole situation more difficult to fight.

Election frauds are arguably the worst form of political corruption, because their objective is to interfere with the democratic process that is integral to the government of the United States. Elections can be controlled in two ways: through party workers and through election officials. Crimes such as ballot-box stuffing, false or non-registration of voters, deliberate miscount-

Sam Giancana   Vito Genovese   John Scalish   Raymond Patria

John S. LaRocca   Angelo Bruno   Stefano Magaddino   Joseph Zeri

The above notorious heads of organized crime, though guilty of many white-collar crimes, are better known for more menacing offenses.

ing, and disregard of absentee ballots are a threat to the democratic way of life.

Bankruptcy frauds are a common white-collar corporate crime. These frauds are sometimes known as "bustouts" or "planned bankruptcies." It is a felony to transfer property of a corporation that is in contemplation of bankruptcy. The purpose of U.S. bankruptcy law is to protect an insolvent debtor from harassment by creditors. But it also protects lawful creditors. The law forbids a debtor—a person or a business—to hide assets and property from creditors or from bankruptcy court. One way for corporations to hide their property from creditors and from bankruptcy court is to sell or transfer that property to some other corporation. Since hiding corporate assets requires skillful tricks by corporate officers and accountants, this is considered a white-collar crime known as bankruptcy fraud. The guilty officers cover their tracks by destroying or falsifying company records that might reveal where assets were sold or were hidden. It is up to the creditors to initiate involuntary bankruptcy proceedings, and they must be able to prove that the firm is insolvent. But it is difficult for creditors to act quickly in court when they suspect illegal concealment or sale of corporate assets.

Bankruptcy frauds usually follow one of the following four patterns, according to author August Bequai— the "similar name" scam, the "old company" technique, the "new company" technique, and the "successful business" scam. The similar name scam involves creating a new corporation. By law the name must not be in use already—so the new corporation is given a name very similar to an established corporation's name. The similar name can trick suppliers into doing business on credit with the new corporation.

The second method is when an "old" company decides to "turn scam" and make a quick profit. The decision could be based on financial difficulties, but usually the company has taken on silent partners, possibly persons involved in organized crime.

The third technique is when a new company is formed as a "front." When the new company receives its orders for merchandise purchased on credit, the merchandise is distributed and the money pocketed. The "front" disappears quickly when unpaid creditors begin to suspect fraud. This is similar to the "shell company" technique some businesses use to obtain a contract with the government through the federal Small Business Administration.

In the fourth method, the "successful business" scam, the ownership or management of a successful company changes, and the new owners or managers use the good reputation of the business to pocket all the money they can. Eventually the business goes bankrupt.

The crimes we associate with "gangsters"—murder, kidnapping, and other violent crimes—are not considered white collar. But mob figures use other illegal practices to infiltrate legitimate businesses. Title IX of the federal Organized Crime Control Act of 1970 is a very powerful law known as RICO (Racketeer Influenced and Corrupt Organizations Act). This law was designed to prevent organized crime from mixing with legitimate business.

RICO makes racketeering a federal offense and provides stiff penalties—up to $20,000 in fines and up to 20 years in prison. Persons convicted of certain charges under RICO could also be required to forfeit any assets gained from illegal activities. "Racketeering" is defined as having 32 "predicate" offenses, including murder, gambling, arson, bribery, extortion (especially for "protection" money), drug dealing, embezzlement from pension or welfare funds, and bankruptcy fraud. Other activities have been added to RICO: trafficking in contraband cigarettes (sales tax not paid), state or federal obscenity violations, child pornography, and money laundering.

In many major U.S. cities, organized crime syndicates or "families" control trucking; loading and unloading of trucks, planes, and ships; the building and contracting industries; shipping, sanitation and waste removal; food distributors, food processors, and grocers; the importing and exporting of legal and illegal goods; labor unions; local politics; and in some cases, even law enforcement. Organized crime members use fraud, extortion, bribery, embezzlement, and threats of bodily harm to run these businesses at enormous profits. Since

Charles Keating Jr. was one of the lead figures tried in the savings and loan failures of the late 1980s.

racketeers infiltrate legal businesses more often by using accountants and lawyers than by using force or violence, their actions are really white-collar crimes, too. Today's "mobster" sometimes wears a white shirt and necktie when he goes to "work."

In *Bilking Bankers and Bad Debts*, authors Henry Pontell and Kitty Calavita describe the notorious savings and loan crisis of the late 1980s and early 1990s. Thousands of savings and loans went bankrupt—many of them because of criminal actions by the owners and managers.

Some savings and loans failed legitimately because

of continuous poor management. But fraud caused a high percentage of the failures. Many savings and loans failed because of exorbitant bonuses or salary raises for CEOs and other officials, the use of business funds to buy private planes or vacation homes, excessive and high-risk loans, and faulty accounting. All of these practices led to business failures that cost many savings and loan depositors their life savings. Some of these actions were intentional and therefore criminal. Other savings and loan officials were guilty of nothing more than incredibly bad business sense. Some, too, may have had connections to organized crime.

Each instance of embezzlement, unlawful risk-taking when investing depositors' funds, and covering up the evidence is a separate crime. Often one kind of white-collar crime does not occur without several others. If you embezzled $10,000 from your business for personal use, you would probably try to keep others from finding out by falsifying the account books or receipts. If you knew other people knew about it, you might bribe or blackmail them to keep quiet about it. And if you didn't get caught, you might keep doing it. Each time you embezzle, each time you lie in the accounts, each time you bribe or extort is a separate crime for which you could be prosecuted. One white-collar crime frequently leads to another.

Monopolies were a problem in this country until federal antitrust laws were passed to prevent the corruption of a free marketplace, an economic principle on which the United States was founded. If a company creates a monopoly to control an entire industry, it can eliminate its competition and demand exorbitant prices for its goods or services because it is the only seller. These antitrust laws try to prevent that.

One of the most famous federal antitrust laws is the Sherman Antitrust Act of 1890. Others include the Clayton Act of 1914 and the Federal Trade Commission Act of 1914. These allowed for the creation of

Members of the Environmental Protection Agency test samples of toxic waste abandoned at a factory in Pennsylvania.

state fair-trade laws and established the Federal Trade Commission (FTC).

Other agencies that enforce antitrust laws and oversee segments of the economy include the Interstate Commerce Commission, the Securities and Exchange Commission, and the Civil Aeronautics Board. These agencies were established because the federal antitrust laws left vast loopholes and provided for many exemptions. For example, labor unions and agricultural groups are exempt from certain articles of the acts.

The federal antitrust statutes can be enforced by private individuals, by the states, by the Federal Trade Commission, and by the federal Justice Department. In 1973, the state of New Jersey, according to August Bequai, "charged more than twelve national firms and over one hundred local firms with violations of the antitrust laws."

Yet another corporate crime involves environmental offenses such as illegally polluting air, water, or land or adversely altering the environment. The relevant laws against these crimes include the Rivers and Harbors Appropriations Act of 1899, the National Environmental Policy Act of 1969, the Environmental Quality Improvement Act of 1970, and the Federal Pollution Control Act. The Clean Air Act of 1965 established the Environmental Protection Agency (EPA) to investigate alleged misconduct. The EPA is empowered to bring criminal violators of environmental laws to justice. Individual states have also passed environmental protection laws.

Here, too, organized crime has infiltrated. Where the mob controls trucking, truckers have been accused of illegally dumping toxic materials. Violation of federal and state environmental laws is white-collar crime that benefits businesses and the people who do the unlawful dumping of toxic waste and dangerous chemicals. Treating industrial waste to make it legal for disposal can cost tens of millions of dollars. That cost is

greatly reduced if a corporation pays an illegal service to haul away the waste and dump it in our rivers or landfills. The business saves a fortune and the illegal dumpers make money. Unfortunately, the cost of environmental damage is often incalculable.

Many corporate crimes have taken place in the securities trade. The first securities exchange, the New York Stock Exchange or NYSE, was established by agreement between stockbrokers in 1792. The American Stock Exchange (AMEX), originally called the Curb Exchange because its members met in the streets, was established in the mid-1800s. Both of these exchanges, and others founded later, have self-

The New York Stock Exchange, the nation's first securities exchange, was established in 1792. Investment scams followed soon after.

David Silverman pleaded guilty to insider stock trading and securities fraud in 1986.

regulatory bodies and rules. When the stock market crashed in 1929, Congress passed the Securities Act of 1933 and the Securities Exchange Act of 1934.

There are several ways for a stockbroker to make illegal fortunes. "Churning" means buying and selling the same stock repeatedly to generate huge sales commissions for the broker. The investor's investment quickly disappears, while the stockbroker has made a fortune on commissions. The stockbroker just channels the investor's money into his own paycheck.

Buying or selling stock without the investor's consent is also illegal. Sometimes a broker is given oral permission by the client to buy or sell. An investor may find that it's his word against his broker's word. In these cases, it is sometimes hard to prove that the broker's behavior was criminal.

A stockbroker may deliberately misrepresent the value of stock to drive the price up or down. He may claim that Company A's stock is bound to go up in price and convince his client to buy it, while he knows that Company A is actually on the verge of bankruptcy and the stock will be worthless. Or, a stockbroker may say that Company A's stock is on its way down in value, knowing that it is not. By convincing people to sell, he or his colleagues can buy it all at a cheaper price.

Counterfeit stock certificates have played a role in many scams. Stock certificates can be used as collateral by banks that will extend credit or cash loans to the owner of the stock. This is what "the Match King," Ivar Kreuger, did. Counterfeiting certificates is a common way for white-collar criminals to raise money by presenting themselves as wealthy businesspeople.

Insider trading is a fraud involving the misuse of confidential information. For example, an assistant general manager at Company X knows that Company X has discovered oil and that the price of its shares is going to increase in value. This information is not yet public and is available only to "insiders." The manager buys stock in Company X before the company announces it has found oil. He also calls his friends at ABC Company to tell them to buy Company X stock. Using valuable, nonpublic information in stock trading is a form of white-collar crime.

Ivan Boesky was convicted of insider trading and went to prison in 1987. He was also barred for life from Wall Street. One writer claims, however, that Boesky is

Wall Street investor Ivan Boesky leaves court after being sentenced to three years in prison for insider trading.

"back in business, managing close to $1 billion on Wall Street for various clients through a Netherlands Antilles shell company." Technically, Boesky is trading on the international market, but such a line of work entails working with, if not on, Wall Street.

Two of the most common white-collar crimes are tax fraud and tax evasion, committed by individuals as well as corporations. It is important to note that tax "avoidance" is not a crime. A corporation or an individual taxpayer may bend the state and federal tax codes to the legal limit. If they should underpay their taxes, then the state or the federal Internal Revenue Service will assess against them a civil penalty for underpayment. But deliberately filing a false tax return or deliberately concealing taxable income is a crime of either tax evasion or fraud.

Not surprisingly, many suspected organized crime figures, with enormous illegal incomes, are listed as earning some ridiculously low amounts of income on their tax returns. If tax fraud is suspected, the federal government steps in to investigate. The investigation can lead to discovery of other crimes as well, or it can be one way to prosecute organized crime figures. The famous gangster Al Capone was finally arrested, charged, convicted, and imprisoned but only for the crime of tax evasion.

The National White Collar Crime Center provides national support for the prevention, investigation, and prosecution of white-collar and economic crimes. The NWCCC counts state and local law enforcement officials, regulatory agencies, and prosecutors as its members. It provides free services to its members, such as computer database sharing, analytical services, case funding, training, and research. The NWCCC claims to have assisted in recovering over $349 million in restitution, $29 million in fines, $4 million in recovered property, and $330 million for the IRS, recovered from tax fraud cases.

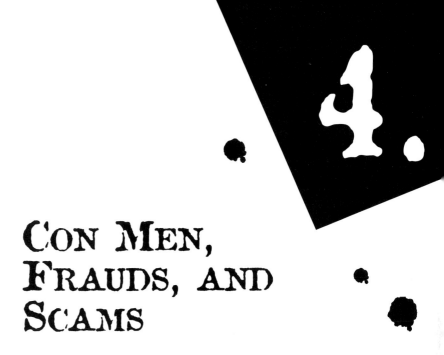

Con Men, Frauds, and Scams

*In 1959, an elderly man was found seriously ill in a hotel room in Connecticut. He had registered as "Dr. B. A. Morris." The hotel staff had him taken to a hospital, where the man died the next day. In their attempts to notify the man's next of kin, the hotel staff discovered that Dr. Morris was really Frederick Emerson Peters, a "gentleman" con man. The FBI had been looking for him for years.

Peters had spent days perfecting bad checks only to make off quietly with small change. Once, he told a store clerk that he wished to purchase a gift for his daughter that cost $97.63. He gave the clerk a worthless check for $100, asked that his gift be mailed to his daughter, and left without the merchandise, pocketing only the change from his bad check—$2.37.

Peters was unusually knowledgeable. When he impersonated surgeons, he knew what medical equipment he would need for his operating room. When he

Before computers, white-collar crime was often committed with pen and ink, but it employed the same creativity and cunning that today's white-collar criminals use.

Violinist Fritz Kreisler passed off his compositions as lost works by some of the great composers.

went to rare book shops, he knew about rare first editions and unusual print styles. When he went to an Oriental antiques shop, he knew about dynasties of ancient China. This knowledge helped him appear to be an expert. But this is not why he was so hard to catch. As an FBI agent said, "The old rascal charms his victims and hits them so light, lots of them don't even make a complaint."

There have been other perpetrators of hoaxes who, like Peters, had motives other than large financial gain. Fritz Kreisler, a critically acclaimed concert violinist who died in 1962, was also a composer. But the pieces he composed were presented by Kreisler as "lost works" by famous composers such as Antonio Vivaldi, Gaetano Pugnani, François Couperin, Niccolo Porpora, and Padre Martini. "I just wanted some pieces for myself, and I

wrote them," he said later. "I was 18 and wanted to be a violinist, not a composer. I wanted to give recitals and I couldn't put several pieces on the program and sign them all 'Kreisler.' It would have looked arrogant." Kreisler never made very much money off his forgeries, but he did always request that whenever the pieces were played, his name be mentioned as their editor.

Another artist managed to fool art critics for a decade. His scheme was uncovered almost by accident. After World War II, a painting by the famous Dutch master Jan Vermeer was discovered in the collection of Hermann Göring, Adolf Hitler's air marshal. A Dutch painter, Hans van Meegeren, had sold it to the Nazis. To the Dutch, oppressed by the invading German army, the sale to the enemy of a priceless national treasure was worse than treason.

Artist Hans van Meegeren (above) at work on a perfect copy of Vermeer's painting Jesus Teaching in the Temple. *He painted it in front of six witnesses to prove to the world his claim that that he could forge a masterpiece.*

Under police interrogation, van Meegeren confessed that this painting and five others he had sold were forgeries. Controversy raged across Europe as critics stood by their earlier statements that the paintings were authentic. Van Meegeren proved the truth of his confession by painting another fake Vermeer under police supervision.

The forgery was physically foolproof. Van Meegeren had used linen from Vermeer's time, made his own oil paints in the same manner as Vermeer had, and made his own brushes in Vermeer's own way. He had even scratched tiny cracks in the paintings and baked them in an oven to simulate the way Vermeer's paintings had cracked with age. Van Meegeren was an artist in more ways than one.

But van Meegeren did not forge these paintings for the money alone. He had been a successful artist in his own right until a bitter feud with Dutch critics, when van Meegeren refused to pay them for good reviews. So in 1936, van Meegeren had gotten even with the critics by duping them. Whatever his original goals, van Meegeren did make himself rich in the process, earning over $3 million.

Some white-collar criminals engage in mail fraud schemes, offering cash prizes or vacations, real estate, artwork, insurance, rare coins or gems, or investment opportunities that actually provide much less than was advertised. An article in Modern Maturity magazine cited some memorable mail fraud examples. Hide-A-Swat was guaranteed to kill flies and pests for only $9.95—it was only a rolled-up newspaper. A solar clothes dryer was an old-fashioned clothes line and clothespins. An advertised universal coat hanger for only $3.99 was a 10¢ nail.

Many mail and telemarketing scams target senior citizens. "Persons 65 and older constitute up to 30 percent of all fraud victims, even though they are approximately 12 percent of the population," says the FBI

Barry Minkow, once convicted and sentenced to jail for fraud, talks on a radio program about fraud and how to prevent it.

Crime Squad home page. Many states have recently instituted crime-prevention or fraud-prevention organizations that work to get the word out among senior citizens and others. The Federal Trade Commission has compiled a Telemarketing Fraud Database, which keeps information about frauds and swindlers on file for government and law enforcement agencies.

But home-repair or home-improvement scams, investment scams, and car-repair scams can happen to anyone. Like the Williamsons discussed in chapter 2, who installed fake lightning rods on houses, other swindlers offer to reseal driveways or repair roofs. Then they either take a deposit and never do the job, or, like the Williamsons, use shoddy or useless materials, sometimes ruining the original driveway or roof. Other home-improvement or auto-repair swindlers offer to inspect a house or car for free, and then recommend unnecessary repairs.

Investment scams are everywhere, as well. They come in the mail, over the phone, in advertisements, in printed media, with fake referrals, or from "shell" offices—not to mention all the investment frauds that occur on the stock market. Investment scams are quite capable of stripping the victims of their life savings and putting them in overwhelming debt. The FBI Crime Squad notes that there are many different schemes, including offers for the sale of land, time-shares, commodities and futures trading, franchises, financial planning services, gold and silver, rare coins, and oil and gas leases.

One famous con artist who defrauded his victims of more than $100 million now works to inform people about fraud prevention. Barry Minkow, who at age 16 was CEO of one of the fastest-growing companies on Wall Street, pleaded guilty in late 1987 to no fewer than 57 counts of fraud. Sentenced in 1989 to a quarter century in jail, he was ordered to restore $26 million of the money he stole.

Since his conversion to Christianity in jail and his parole in 1995, Minkow has written several books about his own crimes and how to avoid similar fraudulent schemes. He gives lectures on the topic to corporate executives, lawyers, and law-enforcement officials. Writer Christopher Byron notes that "today, Minkow would probably be a safer person with whom to invest than a good many brokers and advisers on Wall Street," even though Minkow himself says, "I'm really no good with money."

On the other hand, Michael Milken, known as the merger- and junk-bond king, is apparently back at his old job. Milken pleaded guilty to six counts of securities law violations in 1990. He spent 22 months in prison

Michael Milken leaves court while on trial for charges of fraud and racketeering.

and was barred by the Securities and Exchange Commission from investment advising or consulting. That prohibition, however, does not bar him from going into business for himself and doing general business consulting.

Since the dishonest stockbroker or home repair person is not committing a violent crime, such frauds are regarded as white collar because the real crime entails violating the trust of victims. White-collar criminals dress in business suits or coveralls, but their crimes are the same—they take advantage of those of us who believe in them and in their scams.

PREVENTION AND PUNISHMENT

How should white-collar criminals be punished? Are they being punished too leniently, or too harshly? How can we measure the effect white-collar crimes have on society, on our collective sense of security, on our economy? And is the term *white-collar crime* even a meaningful phrase? Is there really a distinction between white-collar and other crimes? And how can we stop potential white-collar criminals from committing crimes in the first place?

Many cases of white-collar crime are intricate, play out over long periods, involve dozens of separate crimes, have multiple defendants, and involve violations of complex laws. Because of the difficulty in prosecuting these cases, the best way to deter white-collar

Bearing in mind the words over the U.S. Supreme Court building, judges must decide the proper punishments for white-collar crimes in order to give "equal justice under law."

65

In an electronic age, physically securing cash from armed robbers isn't enough. White-collar criminals can steal millions with a computer and a modem.

criminals is to prevent them from being able to commit their crimes in the first place.

Increased public awareness of fraudulent schemes is the best prevention for consumers. When presented with a possible scam, ask for credentials. Ask for time to decide. Ask for information to be sent to you. Get all the facts before sending or even offering money. Be wary of charming strangers offering get-rich-quick schemes. If you are unfamiliar with the company, check its credentials with your local Better Business Bureau before dealing with it. If you have received a mail-order offer, you can check with the U.S. Post Office to see if there are any complaints about the offering company. You cannot be too careful.

A great deal of corporate crime is commited from the inside. Increased security at companies cannot be limited to "outsiders" if fraud and embezzlement are to be prevented. If there is sensitive information or an unusual amount of cash accessible to too many employees, perhaps corporate responsibility should be limited to fewer, more trustworthy people. Also, people cannot be too trusting of their fellow employees.

Awareness can help prevent a person or company from becoming a victim, but it is not likely that white-collar crimes will disappear entirely. Enforcement of laws, prosecution, and punishment are obviously necessary. Even with all the questions they raise, cases like that of Kevin Mitnick may be the easy ones to judge. Solving other white-collar crimes and bringing other white-collar criminals to justice can be much more problematic. Embezzlement, forgery, bribery, extortion, and fraud are certainly crimes. They result in billions of lost dollars every year, and they undermine everyone's faith in their fellow humans and in the economy. But just how to deal with white-collar crime remains a criminal-justice puzzle.

Many savings and loan fraud cases, for example, have not made it to trial because of difficulties in gathering evidence and limited resources of enforcement agencies. Even in the high-profile cases that did result in convictions, the penalties imposed often looked light compared to the damage done. The notorious savings and loan kingpin Donald Dixon was convicted of 23 counts of fraud, costing U.S. taxpayers a total of $1.3 billion. Yet Dixon was sentenced to just five years in prison. How do judges decide?

There is great debate among judges, prosecutors, defenders, and other law-enforcement professionals as to how severely, or leniently, white-collar criminals should be punished. In *Sitting in Judgment*, authors Stanton Wheeler, Kenneth Mann, and Austin Sarat explore the sentencing of white-collar criminals compared to the punishment given to those who commit violent crimes. Do judges in this country share the same sentencing standards?

Most judges and most ordinary citizens view white-collar criminals as being less threatening to society than violent criminals. As one judge remarks in *Sitting in Judgment*, "The person who embezzles ten grand is not likely to get the same penalty as somebody who walks into a bank with a submachine gun and robs it of ten grand. . . . Going to a bank and holding a gun to somebody is more serious than embezzlement."

But what if the amount of money is much higher in the embezzlement case? What if the embezzler stole $10 million and the bank robber $10,000? A different judge states, "There may be more money [in a price-fixing case] but you don't have these long-lasting traumatic effects on the individual that you do where a robber comes into a bank and puts a gun in a teller's face and the teller doesn't forget it for a number of years."

Sometimes, white-collar crimes are called "victimless," not because the crime hurts no one, but because it is much more difficult to assess who is the criminal and who is the victim. In civil cases of white-collar crime, sometimes the "victim" is just as guilty as the person he or she is suing.

Since the effects on the victims of white-collar crime are harder to identify than are the effects on victims of violent crime, judges use several distinguishing characteristics. One is the amount of money stolen. If the amount was over $100,000, the authors of *Sitting in Judgment* find, most judges are likely to give a harsher sentence than if it was only a thousand dollars. Simi-

Charles Keating Jr. takes the oath prior to testifying at his trial. He eventually was sentenced to 10 years in prison for his part in a savings and loan failure.

larly, if the money was stolen from relatively helpless individuals—such as older people being bilked out of their life savings—most judges will hand down a stiffer penalty than if the funds came from a large corporation or from the federal government itself. The nature of the victim, then, also affects the penalty.

The duration of the crime also affects the sentence. If the crime involved a high degree of deliberation and repeated offenses occurring over a long period of time, the judge is more likely to increase the individual's term in prison. Finally, judges assess the violation of trust

In assessing the appropriate punishment for white-collar criminals, judges weigh various factors, including the duration of the offense, the professional standing of the offender, and the vulnerability of the victims.

that occurs in white-collar offenses. Many white-collar criminals are in a position of trust. In cases involving elected officials, physicians, military officials, government employees, law enforcement personnel (including judges), priests and ministers, and others who bear a high degree of responsibility in their positions, judges are likely to sentence more heavily. This extra burden may seem unfair to some, but the authors of *Sitting in Judgment* explain: "This heightened concern for trust and trust violation reflects more than the common sense moral judgement that persons in responsible positions have a special obligation to behave responsibly. There is a sense that their violations damage the fabric of society in a way that others, even those who may employ violence as a means to their ends, do not. . . . Thus, violation of a position of trust is seen to have an impact far beyond the immediate victims."

One example of these kinds of violations is election fraud, which attacks the basis of democratic government itself. This has a harsher effect on the "fabric of society" than does the crime of someone who falsifies the records of a large steel corporation to cover his or her theft.

But judges cannot assess only the offense. They must assess the offender too. The person may have been ultimately responsible for the crime being committed, but did he or she realize it was illegal? Did he or she realize the consequences? Was the crime intentional? In other words, how worthy of punishment is this person?

One way for judges to assess the culpability of a person is to take into account whether he or she already has a criminal record reflecting the same type of crime. Just as an armed robber with two prior convictions for armed robbery is likely to get a stiff sentence, so is the con man who has been convicted of fraud already. But the overwhelming majority of white-collar criminals are first-time offenders. What do judges rely on to sentence those offenders?

One thing judges look for is knowledge and intent. Were the illegal actions knowingly and willfully undertaken? How deliberate was the crime? How much scheming did the offense involve? Sometimes it is difficult to tell. One judge interviewed for *Sitting in Judgment* said, "There are situations . . . where a guy definitely didn't pay all the taxes he owed, but . . . was it really willful fraud or was it just sloppy bookkeeping; maybe in some vague sense that maybe I'm not paying everything I owe, but I'm probably pretty close, and then it turns out you were $30,000 off. Is it that kind of a case, or is there just no doubt that this guy knew?"

The crime still exists and the person is still guilty, but most judges feel the sentence for the first scenario, the "sloppy" one, should be lighter than for the other, the person man who knew.

Stockbroker Richard John Byrd was sentenced to one year in prison and ordered to pay $273,000 after his conviction on forgery charges.

In many white-collar crime cases there is more than one defendant. In these cases, judges try to assess the relative culpability of the offenders. The mastermind is likely to get a heavier sentence than the person he or she got to assist him. If there are few or no differences in degree of culpability, all the convicted get the same sentence.

An accused person's character and life history, and even his or her present circumstances, can be a "yardstick" for sentencing. This yardstick hearkens back to whether the criminal is in a position of trust in his or her community or career. Judges usually weigh the positive, exemplary past behavior of a person when deciding on the sentence, just as they weigh the negative past behavior, such as repeated offenses.

Judges are not likely to give a light sentence to a flagrant white-collar offender just because he or she comes from a wealthy background or had many privileges growing up. In fact, some judges give stiffer sentences to these persons. But it is important to note that the idea of punishment for white-collar criminals is different from that for "common criminals."

Rapists, murderers, or armed robbers are sent to prison not just as punishment for what they have done, but to prevent them from raping, killing, or robbing again. Drug smugglers are imprisoned not only to punish them, but to prevent more drugs from reaching more people. Incarceration prevents a violent criminal from committing another violent crime. Ideally the prisoner is rehabilitated in prison and, when released, will not commit another violent crime. For white-collar criminals, incarceration is primarily punishment, not prevention. Often he or she doesn't need to be locked up to prevent the crime from being committed again, as many white-collar criminals are extremely unlikely to do so.

Punishment of white-collar criminals is also important for deterrence—to prevent others who might be tempted from committing that crime. Some judges interviewed in *Sitting in Judgment* comment: "If any kind of crime is deterrable, it ought to be [white-collar crime]. The guy who sits down and makes out his income tax, he is engaging in a rather deliberate, purposive, thoughtful act, and he is appraising the consequences. [Another judge says] I think a lot of people decide to pay their taxes so they won't go to jail. [Still another:] It is clear in white-collar cases people have more to lose [by going to jail]. More to lose in the way of reputation, more to lose in the way of money, more to lose in the way of family ties." For these people, being indicted, charged, and possibly tried can almost be punishment enough. They are sentenced nonetheless. Deterrence is effective for most white-collar criminals.

The idea of motive is not ignored either. Did the person commit his crime through need or greed? Is the embezzler trying to support four children alone? Is the person trying to pay for nursing-home care for her mother and pay the mortgage and the insurance? Or is the thief already fairly wealthy? Is the thief a professional con artist and habitual criminal? Did he cover up his crime, or worse, lie on the witness stand? One judge says that covering up and lying are "an attempt, if you will, to continue the crime." Another says, "If a person is contrite and admits what he has done, he is less likely to get a prison sentence. I might say that is true of blue-collar crime also, if the fellow has no prior record. If a person has a prior record, you have a right to assume that his protestations are not sincere."

Sometimes, white-collar criminals are sentenced to make restitution of the money they stole. Sentencing a criminal to pay back the victims is generally an effective way of punishing and also rehabilitating him or her. One judge interviewed in *Sitting in Judgment* recalls a case in which a man convicted of securities fraud offered to pay back all the money the victims had lost. This amount was nearly twice the profit the thief himself had made. The judge put him on probation, not in prison.

Barry Minkow was sentenced to prison and required to make restitution of $26 million—an unusually high amount, although it was only a portion of the $100 million he stole. Minkow served seven years in jail, behaving so well that the judge who sentenced him encouraged his parole.

Similarly, white-collar criminals might be sentenced to community service rather than prison. It has been argued that this is because judges, who are often from

middle- or upper-class backgrounds, empathize with white-collar criminals. However, this situation may be due more to the skills of the white-collar criminals themselves. That is, they are usually well educated and can contribute their expertise and skills to the community they have offended. Also, community service is usually given in conjunction with another punishment such as restitution, a short jail sentence, or probation.

White-collar crimes will always be with us, whatever term we use to describe them. They may even increase because of increased access to computers. Prevention, awareness, and continued prosecution and punishment remain the only responses to these crimes.

Attorney General Janet Reno announces criminal charges against 11 brokers who swindled elderly investors out of millions of dollars in assets.

Bibliography

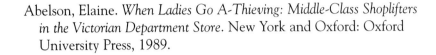

Abelson, Elaine. *When Ladies Go A-Thieving: Middle-Class Shoplifters in the Victorian Department Store*. New York and Oxford: Oxford University Press, 1989.

Bequai, August. *White-Collar Crime: A Twentieth Century Crisis*. Lexington, Mass., and Toronto: DC Heath and Co., 1978.

Byron, Christopher. "$26 Million in the Hole." *Worth* (March 1996).

———. "Happily Ever After." *Esquire* (April 1995).

Chua-Eoan, Howard G. "Going for Broke." *Time* (March 13, 1995).

Corley, Eric. "Free the Hacker Two." *Harper's Magazine* (September 1989): 22–25.

Elliott, Michael. "Nick Leeson, Meet Carlo Ponzi." *Newsweek* (March 13, 1995): 47.

Gill, Mark Stuart. "Cybercops Take a Byte out of Crime." *Smithsonian* (May 1997).

Hafner, Katie. "Morris Code." *New Republic* (February, 19, 1990).

"Immigrants Swindle Their Own." *New York Times*, August 24, 1992.

Katz, Leon. *Ill-Gotten Gains: Evasion, Blackmail, Fraud and Kindred Puzzles of the Law*. Chicago and London: University of Chicago Press, 1996.

Lane, Randall. "Back in Action." *Forbes* (July 17, 1995): 46–48.

Lipman, Mark. *Stealing: How America's Employees Are Stealing Their Companies Blind*. New York: Harper's Magazine Press, 1973.

Machlis, Sharon. "Phone Hackers Dial up Trouble." *Computerworld* (February 24, 1997).

Meyer, Michael. "Is This Hacker Evil or Merely Misunderstood: Two Writers Clash over the Crimes of Kevin Mitnick." *Newsweek* (December 4, 1995).

Powell, Bill. "Busted!" *Newsweek* (March 13, 1995).

Reader's Digest Association. *Scoundrels and Scalawags: 51 Stories of the Most Fascinating Characters of Hoax and Fraud.* Pleasantville, N.Y.: The Reader's Digest Association, 1968.

Scheier, Robert. "Lock the Damned Door!" *Computerworld* (February 10, 1997).

Schlegel, Kip, and David Weisburd, eds. *White-Collar Crime Reconsidered.* Boston: Northeastern University Press, 1992.

Sussman, Vic. "Policing Cyberspace." *U.S. News and World Report* (January 23, 1995).

Sutherland, Edwin. *White Collar Crime.* New York: Dryden Press, 1949.

Viles, Peter. "Hackers Plead Guilty in Contest Fraud." *Broadcasting and Cable* (May 3, 1993).

Wanat, Thomas. "Two Internet-Savvy Students Help Track Down Hacker." *Chronicle of Higher Education,* March 1997, p. A30.

Wheeler, Stanton; Kenneth Mann; and Austin Sarat. *Sitting in Judgment: The Sentencing of White-Collar Criminals.* New Haven and London: Yale University Press, 1988.

Worsnop, Richard. "Mafia Crackdown." *CQ Researcher* (March 27, 1992).

White-Collar Crime Websites

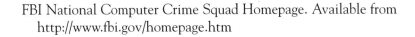

FBI National Computer Crime Squad Homepage. Available from
http://www.fbi.gov/homepage.htm

The Law Office Consumer Guide. Available from
http://www.thelawoffice.com/LLA/IL/C13.HTM.#160

National White Collar Crime Center. Available from
http://www.iir.com/nwccc/nwccc.htm

Index

GINA DE ANGELIS was born and raised in Hershey, Pennsylvania. She holds a B.A. from Marlboro College, Vermont, and an M.A. from the University of Mississippi. She lives in Williamsburg, Virginia. This is her ninth book for Chelsea House.

AUSTIN SARAT is William Nelson Cromwell Professor of Jurisprudence and Political Science at Amherst College, where he also chairs the Department of Law, Jurisprudence and Social Thought. Professor Sarat is the author or editor of 23 books and numerous scholarly articles. Among his books are *Law's Violence*, *Sitting in Judgment: The Sentencing of White-Collar Criminals*, and *Justice and Injustice in Law and Legal Theory*. He has received many academic awards and held several prestigious fellowships. He is President of the Law & Society Association and Chair of the Working Group on Law, Culture and the Humanities. In addition, he is a nationally recognized teacher and educator whose teaching has been featured in the *New York Times*, on the *Today* show, and on National Public Radio's *Fresh Air*.

Picture Credits